I0485469

How To Organize A Successful Speech

How to put together a speech that will capture and hold your audience's attention

"Practical, proven techniques that will help you to make your next speech a success"

Dr. Jim Anderson

How To Organize A Successful Speech: How To Put Together A Speech That Will Clearly Communicate Your Message To Your Audience
Jim Anderson

Copyright 2017 by Jim Anderson

Kindle Edition

Published by:
Blue Elephant Consulting
Tampa, Florida

Printed in the United States of America

Library of Congress Control Number: 2017903645

ISBN-13: 978-1517613136
ISBN-10: 1517613132

Recent Books By The Author

Product Management

- Marketing Skills For Product Managers

- How Product Managers Can Grow Their Career: How Product Managers Can Find And Succeed In The Right Job

Public Speaking

- How To Become A Better Speaker By Changing How You Speak: Change techniques that will transform a speech into a memorable event

- How To Give A Great Presentation: Presentation techniques that will transform a speech into a memorable event

CIO Skills

- What CIOs Need To Know About Working With Partners: Techniques For CIOs To Use In Order To Be Able To Successfully Work With Partners

- How CIOs Can Make Innovation Happen: Tips And Techniques For CIOs To Use In Order To Make Innovation Happen In Their IT Department

IT Manager Skills

- How IT Managers Can Make Innovation Happen: Tips And Techniques For IT Managers To Use In Order To Make Innovation Happen In Their Teams

- Secrets Of Effective Leadership For IT Managers: Tips And Techniques That IT Managers Can Use In Order To Develop Leadership Skills

Negotiating

- Learn How To Signal In Your Next Negotiation: How To Develop The Skill Of Effective Signaling In A Negotiation In Order To Get The Best Possible Outcome

- Learn The Skill Of Exploring In A Negotiation: How To Develop The Skill Of Exploring What Is Possible In A Negotiation In Order To Reach The Best Possible Deal

Miscellaneous

- The Internet-Enabled Successful School District Superintendent: How To Use The Internet To Boost Parental Involvement In Your Schools

- Power Distribution Unit (PDU) Secrets: What Everyone Who Works In A Data Center Needs To Know!

Note: See a complete list of books by Dr. Jim Anderson at the back of this book.

Acknowledgements

Any book like this one is the result of years of real-world work experience. In my over 25 years of working for 7 different firms, I have met countless fantastic people and I've been mentored by some truly exceptional ones. Although I've probably forgotten some of the people who made me the person that I am today, here is my attempt to finally give them the recognition that they so truly deserve:

- Thomas P. Anderson
- Art Puett
- Bobbi Marshall
- Bob Boggs

Dr. **Jim** Anderson

This book is dedicated to my family: Lori, Maddie, Nick, and Ben. None of this would have been possible without their constant love and support.

Thanks for always believing in me and providing me with the strength to always be willing to go out there and be my best for you.

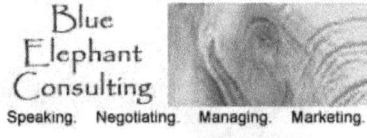

Table of Contents

How To Organize Your Next Speech

The goal of any speaker is that when they give their speech their audience hangs on their every word. In order to make this happen, we need to find ways to organize our speech so that we can both capture and hold our audience's attention from start to finish.

Every speech has to start out well and this is a great opportunity to do some bragging about yourself to your audience. Al Gore has some tips for us so that we can understand what budgets we have to spend during our speech. If you get asked to give more than one speech in a day, you're going to have to know how to manage your voice for the duration.

If you want your next speech to make an impression then you are going to have to find a way to inspire your audience. This all starts with how you plan on going on capturing your audience's attention. Networking with your audience is the key to getting them to listen to what you are going to be telling them.

Everything that you do starts from the moment that the curtain goes up. What your audience thinks of you is often determined by the introduction. If you get asked to deliver a keynote, then you are going to need to get some guidance on how to create and deliver one successfully.

In the end, it's how you choose to organize your speech that will determine the impact that it will have on your audience. Carefully creating a speech that has all of the parts that you are going to need in order to capture your audience's attention is what is going to make your next speech memorable.

For more information on what it takes to be a great public speaker, check out my blog, The Accidental Communicator, at:

www.TheAccidentalCommunicator.com

Good luck!

- Dr. Jim Anderson

About The Author

I must confess that I never set out to be a public speaker. When I went to school, I studied Computer Science and thought that I'd get a nice job programming and that would be that. Well, at least part of that plan worked out!

My first job was working for Boeing on their F/A-18 fighter jet program. I spent my days programming fighter jet software in assembly language and I loved it. The U.S. government decided to save some money and went looking for other countries to sell this plane to. This put me into an unfamiliar role: I started to meet with foreign military officials and I ended up having to give speeches in order to explain what my product did.

Time moved on and so did I. I found myself working for Siemens, the big German telecommunications company. They were making phone switches and selling them to the seven U.S. phone companies. The problem was that the switches were too complicated. Customers couldn't tell the difference between one complicated phone switch from another complicated phone switch. Once again I found myself standing in front of the room giving speeches in order to explain what these complicated machines did and why ours were better than anyone else's.

I've spent over 25 years working as a product manager for both big companies and startups. This has given me an opportunity to do many, many presentations for customers, at conferences, and everywhere in-between.

I now live in Tampa Florida where I spend my time managing my consulting business, Blue Elephant Consulting, teaching college courses at the University of South Florida, and traveling to work with companies like yours to share the knowledge that I have about how to create and deliver powerful and effective speeches.

I'm always available to answer questions and I can be reached at:

Dr. Jim Anderson
Blue Elephant Consulting
Email: jim@BlueElephantConsulting.com
Facebook: http://goo.gl/1TVoK
Web: **www.BlueElephantConsulting.com**

"Unforgettable communication skills that will set your ideas free..."

Create Speeches That Motivate Your Audiences And Get Your Message Heard!

Dr. Jim Anderson is available to provide training and coaching on the topics that are the most important to people who have to speak in public: how can I create a speech that people want to hear and how can I deliver in a way that will allow me to connect with my audience and get my point across to them?

Dr. Anderson believes that in order to both learn and remember what he says, speakers need to laugh. Each one of his speeches is full of fun and humor so that what he says "sticks" with everyone.

Dr. Anderson's Public Speaking Training Includes:

1. How to plan your next speech: pick your purpose and understand your audience.
2. What's the best way to get PowerPoint and Keynote to work with you, not against you?
3. What do you need to do when you are presenting in order to truly connect with your audience?

Dr. Jim Anderson presents over 100 speeches per year. To invite Dr. Anderson to speak at your event, contact him at:

Phone: 813-418-6970 or
Email: jim@BlueElephantConsulting.com

Blue
Elephant
Consulting

Speaking.   Negotiating.   Managing.   Marketing.

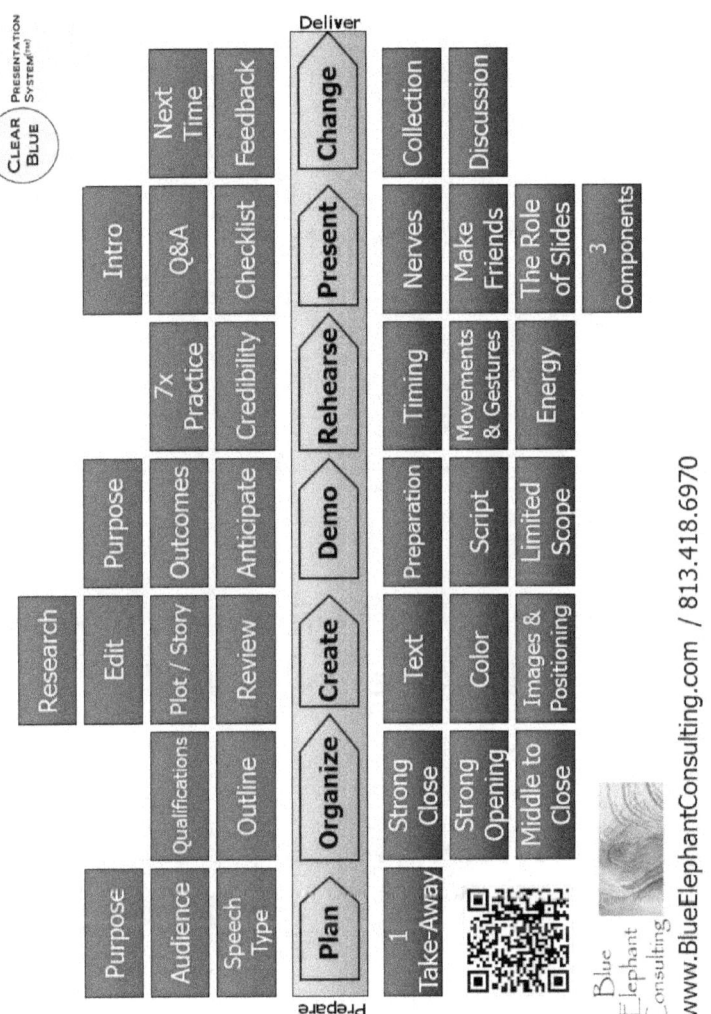

Blue Elephant Consulting has created the **Clear Blue™ Presentation System** for creating and delivering powerful and memorable presentations. The contents of this book are based on lessons learned during the development of the Clear Blue system. Contact Blue Elephant Consulting to learn more about the Clear Blue presentation system.

Chapter 1

Bragging Is What Presenters Need To Be Able To Do Well

Chapter 1: Bragging Is What Presenters Need To Be Able To Do Well

Just in case you've forgotten it, the #1 question on the minds of any audience that is seated and waiting for you to begin talking to them is "**Why should I even bother listening to you?**". This means that in order for you to have any hope of making an impact on this audience, you're going to have to answer this question right off the bat. But how?

The Art Of The Brag

I'm afraid that we're going to have to talk about the "C" word — "**credibility**". As a presenter, it's your job to establish your credibility in the minds of your audience. This is where bragging comes in.

John Spaith has spent some time thinking about how to do this correctly and he's got some good suggestions. Spaith points out that **you always have competition when you give a presentation**. This doesn't mean that you have to deal with other speakers (although sometimes you do), but rather your audience has a lot of other things on their mind and if you don't grab their attention and hold it by establishing your credibility, then they won't pay attention to what you have to say.

A Plan For Self-Promotion (Bragging)

The best way to establish credibility with your audience is to have the person who is introducing you do it for you. However, for a variety of reasons this may not always be possible. When you find yourself in situations like this, **you need to do your bragging yourself**. Here's what Spaith suggests that we think about:

- **Make It Relevant:** If you are addressing a sales team, then spending time talking about the amazing singing career you had in the past won't buy you any credibility.

Instead, make your bragging relevant – tell them that you survived a trip down the Amazon and that you've been shot four times. Survival bragging would work well with this group.

- **It's All Relative:** The accomplishments or talents that you are bragging about have to be something that your audience can relate to. Telling everyone that you are an award winning professional ballroom dancer is great, but who can relate to that? If you tell everyone that you spent 10,000 hours on your feet in uncomfortable shoes practicing to become an award winning professional ballroom dancer, now that's something that we can relate to.

How To Brag

Once you've established **WHAT** you'll be bragging about, you need to nail down just **HOW** you're going to go about doing it. First off, you need to get your bragging done **at the start of your presentation** – credibility is something that you need right off the bat. Next, you need to keep it going long enough to build that credibility, **but not too long**. I'm going to say that a minute should be long enough and you might want to keep it even shorter.

You are going to want to write out and memorize your bragging words. It is so important to get these words just right – not too boastful, but at the same time not too self-deprecating.

Final Thoughts

Some of you might be a bit shy about bragging about yourself – **get over it**. You owe it to your audience to deliver the best presentation that you can and taking the time and effort to make sure that your message sinks in is part of this. Using carefully designed bragging to establish your "street cred" is an important part of any presentation that you give.

Chapter 2

Al Gore Teaches Presenters A Very Convenient Truth

Chapter 2: Al Gore Teaches Presenters A Very Convenient Truth

Interestingly enough, this post has nothing to do with global warming. I really don't care which side of the "warming / not warming" argument you find yourself on right now. The one thing that I think that we can all agree on is that there is quite a debate going on right now – somebody has done a good job of **talking this topic up**!

Grass Roots Speaking

Carl Duivenvoorden cares deeply about global warming issues and has spent time learning about how he can give speeches talking about this topic. If you want to be effective, you go to the source – in this case you go to Al Gore.

Al Gore wrote the book "**An Inconvenient Truth**". He is a skilled and effective public speaker – after all, he's a politician. Lately he has been going around teaching folks how to get the word out about global warming – this means teaching them how to effectively speak in public.

A Speaker's Three Budgets

Al Gore teaches speakers to remember that when they take the stage, they start to spend from **three different budgets** at the same time. They need to accomplish the goal of their speech and get off the stage before they exceed any of their budgets. The three budgets are:

- **Time**: the clock starts ticking when you open your mouth. You always need to respect your audience's time and make sure that you finish on time no matter when you started.

- **Complexity**: there has to be a purpose to your speech – you are not just talking to make people think that you are smart. You have an obligation to make it so that both yourself and your information will be understood (and retained) by your audience.

- **Hope**: this is one that we all too often overlook. We need to carefully plan out the way that our speech will end. We need to make sure that we leave our audience with a sense of being able to change things no matter if we are talking to them about finances or global warming.

Extras That Make A Speech Work

Just doing a great job of speaking often isn't enough. Al Gore teaches that if you want to maximize the impact of your message, you've got to add three additional "**extras**" to your speech in order to make the whole thing work:

- **Use Powerful Visuals**: no, this doesn't mean that you need to create 400 PowerPoint slides. Rather, you need to carefully create just enough visuals to enhance your words – the visuals should echo what you are saying and make your message stick in your audience's mind.

- **Organize Your Visuals**: this should be second nature, but people still do it wrong so it's good to bring it up again: in your visuals, flow your concepts from left to right and top to bottom, use as little text as possible, and give your audience time to focus on the visual as you speak – don't just be whipping through a lot of slides.

- **Worry About The Transitions**: The "flow" of your speech is almost as important as the words that you use. You need to create smooth transitions between the different "chapters" in your speech so that your audience can stay with you from start to finish.

Final Thoughts

No matter what subject you are talking about, you are going to have to use emotion in order to make your message stick. Ultimately your goal is to reach out and touch your audience's hearts. In order to do this you are going to have to use **vocal tones** to draw your audience to you and use your **conviction** and **passion** to connect with your audience. Learn to do this right and you'll be able to intimately connect with your audience and make a **lasting impact** in their lives.

Chapter 3

Back to Back to Back to Back Speaking: How To

Chapter 3: Back to Back to Back to Back Speaking: How To

Just how much speaking can you do in a single day? We spend a lot of time talking about how to prepare for and give a good speech. However, sometimes life just comes at us like a runaway truck and we find ourselves double or triple (or more) booked to speak **in a single day**. Oh oh, looks like we've got a whole new challenge here...

Things To Do The Day Before

Dr. Caren Neile spends a lot of her time speaking to raise funds. She knows a thing or two about **how you've got to prepare** for a day in which you'll be giving multiple speeches.

Dr. Neile points out that your whole day is going to go downhill if you don't **get enough sleep the night before**. This sounds easy to do, but all too often it's not. We rush around the day before we're going to be speaking (writing our speech perhaps?) drinking coffee / tea / soda and then we throw ourselves into our beds, shut our eyes and hope that we'll fall asleep.

Sorry, life doesn't seem to work out that way. All too often when we have a big speaking day ahead of us, we will find ourselves lying in bed completely unable to get to sleep. What you need to do is to make sure that you prepare to have a good night's sleep **at the start of the day before you are going to be speaking**. This means staying away from stimulants (goodbye coffee), getting some exercise in, and basically making sure that you wind things down before you hit the hay. You may still be dealing with nerves, but at least you'll have a better chance of getting to sleep.

Can You Say Siesta?

When was the last time that you took a nap? I'm betting that the last planned nap that you had was **all too long ago** (kindergarten perhaps?). It's time to rediscover the joys of napping.

On a day that you are giving multiple speeches you need to determine if you are going **to be able to fit in naps** in between your speeches. This may strike you as silly, I mean you've got a lot of things that you have to get done that day; however, it turns out that it's one of the best things that you can do and it just might save you from slipping up and saying the wrong thing.

If you take a look at the energy that you'll be expending during a day that you give multiple speeches, **you'll be peaking while you are giving the speeches**. After you've exerted this much energy, you are going to need to recharge your batteries and a nap is a fantastic way to do this. Just remember to wake up before it's time for your next speech!

Drink Heavily!

Sorry, I'm just talking about **drinking water** here. When we speak, the parts of our throat that form the words get dried out. Being hydrated is the key to being able to go the distance in a day in which you'll be doing a lot of speaking.

It probably goes without saying that keeping a glass / bottle of water by your side while you are speaking is also a good idea. This will become even more important as you go through your day and **your body parts start to wear out**.

Eat!

I can't tell you how many times I've seen speakers make one of **two different mistakes** when it comes to eating: either they don't eat at all or they eat too much. Not eating at all is a no-no because you are going to be exerting yourself while you are speaking and if you do this on an empty stomach, you are going to feel the effects. These can range from being distracted by a rumbling stomach to passing out because of low blood sugar. You don't want to do either of these.

Eating too much can cause **similar issues**. One problem is indigestion — who wants to listen to a speaker who keeps burping? The other is that as your body goes to work on all of that food, it's going to boost your body temperature and that's going to slow you down and make you sleepy.

What All Of This Means For You

It would be great if we ran the world, but we don't. This means that sometimes we will find ourselves with commitments to speak **multiple times on a single day**. It can be challenging enough to do a good job giving just one speech, giving multiple speeches in a single day makes life even harder.

The key to doing this well is to make sure that **you prepare to succeed**. This includes getting enough sleep the night before your speeches and then doing the right things as you go through the day of the speeches. Take your time and take care of your body and just like a marathon runner you'll eventually reach the finish line — then you can stop talking!

Chapter 4

You CAN Learn To Speak Like President Obama

Chapter 4: You CAN Learn To Speak Like President Obama

Who do you think is the greatest communicator of all time? For most of us, we'd pick someone who has lived in the last 100 years because that's pretty much all that we know. We've had some great ones in this time period: Winston Churchill, John F. Kennedy, etc. However, if I had to pick **the best communicator** out there right now, I believe that President Obama would win. Now the question for you, independent of your political beliefs, is how can you learn to speak more like him...?

Welcome To The World Of Politics

Linda McGurk spends a lot of time studying how politicians like Obama work their magic, and she's come to some interesting conclusions. The first one is that if you want to have the impact with your speeches that Obama has with his, you are going to have to **learn to be sincere**.

One of the key take-aways from this guidance is that you really do need to **believe in what you are talking about**. Audiences get bombarded with so many different messages these days that they have reacted by developing sophisticated fraud detection capabilities. They can detect if you don't believe the words that you are saying.

Keep in mind that it's not just what you say when you are up in the front of the room or on the stage that counts. Everything that you've done up until that point may be known to the audience and **it counts also**. If you are known to be an avid hunter and you show up to give a speech on why people should be vegetarians, then you are not going to come across as being sincere.

Do You Care, I Mean REALLY Care?

How much **passion** do you have inside of you? Why are you keeping it all bottled up in there? If you want me to listen to you speak about something, you had better be passionate about the topic.

When you let your emotions out, when you let your audience know that you really do care about what you are talking about, that's when you can **connect with them**. It is all too easy to do a great job of researching everything that you need for a speech and then simply delivering a lot of solid facts to your audience. That shows that you care, doesn't it?

The answer is no. If you open up and explain to me why something is important to you, then **I'll listen**. If I can understand how deeply you feel about something then I'll at least listen to you. I may still not agree with you, but I will at least listen.

How Far Can You See: What's Your Vision?

When you are giving a speech, you need to be **painting a picture of the future** for your audience. Once again, if you are just unloading a bunch of facts that you've picked up during your research for this speech, then you won't be able to make a lasting impression.

One of the best examples of a fantastic vision expressed in a speech is John F. Kennedy's **inaugural address** in which he told the country to "ask not what your country can do for you, but what you can do for your country."

This is exactly why people come to hear speeches — they are looking to hear **a vision laid out for them**. This is what makes the good politicians like Obama stand above so many other speakers — they've got the vision thing down cold.

It's All In How You Do It

This all comes back to the basic point: what do you need to do in order to capture some of that politician speaking magic for yourself. There are **three things** that you can do immediately to make your speeches have more of that Obama impact:

- **Have A Conversation:** The more that you are able to work a conversational tone into your speeches, the deeper the connection that you'll be able to make with your audience. Using fancy words or "talking over their heads" will only serve to increase the distance between you and them. Have a conversation with them and you'll be able to make your point.

- **Add Some Punctuation:** Sure, we generally only think about punctuation when we are writing, but politicians show us that it plays a role in our speeches also. Adding periods, semicolons, and new paragraphs to the way that you deliver your speech will allow your audience to catch up and follow along with your thinking.

- **Pause For Effect:** Some of the worst speakers never seem to take a breath when they are speaking. Adding more pauses to your speech is a fantastic way to make it have more of an impact. Pausing allows your audience to laugh, consider a point, or just catch up and ponder what you've just said.

What All Of This Means For You

If you really want to learn how to speak like Obama, then run for the office of President. However, if you need to keep your day job, then perhaps simply **incorporating these suggestions** into your next speech will do the trick.

It turns out that it's **not all that hard to learn to speak like a politician**. The overall goal is to connect with your audience using sincerity, passion, and vision. To do this in your next speech, all you have to do is have a conversation with your audience and add some punctuation and pauses.

I can't guarantee that you'll get elected to an office by incorporating these speaking techniques, but I can assure you that you'll **win the vote** of your next audience.

Chapter 5

Technical Talks: Is There Any Way To Make This Stuff Interesting?

Chapter 5: Technical Talks: Is There Any Way To Make This Stuff Interesting?

I don't know about you, but more and more I've been finding myself being asked to deliver speeches that have technical information in them. I've got a great deal of self-confidence; however, having had to sit through more than my share of boring technical presentations this is the one type of speech that scares me the most. There's got to be a better way...

You Need To Know Your Purpose

Dr. April Andreas has looked into the problem of why technical speeches are so hard to do well and she's discovered that one of the reasons is that all too often we have no idea what we are doing.

Every presentation, including technical presentations, is given for a reason. Before the first word comes out of your mouth, you need to decide why you are standing up there talking. Are you trying to teach your audience? Are you trying to explain your results to them so that they can use them? Are you trying to find that one member of your audience who shares an interest in what you'll be talking about so you can find ways to work with them? Or perhaps your goal is to get people talking about what you've presented and maybe scare up your next job offer.

Be Basic

Congratulations – if you've prepared for your speech, then you really are the smartest person in the room. However, the problem is that not everyone else is as smart as you are. This means that you need to make sure that you don't lose them from the get-go. Dr. Andreas suggests that you make sure that everyone in the room, no matter what their background is, can follow the first 1/3 of your speech. This way when you are done everyone will have gotten something out of listening to you.

How About Some Examples?

Depending on what topic you are talking about (room temperature fusion perhaps?), when you are giving a technical talk things can get pretty detailed very quickly. In order to keep as many people on board for as long as possible, take the time to relate what you are talking about to examples that your audience can find in the real world.

In the case of room temperature fusion, one thing to talk about would be the temperature that fusion normally takes place at which is 119,999,727 degrees Celsius. You could compare this to the temperature at the surface of the sun which is about 6,000 Celsius. Clearly fusion is hot stuff.

Pictures Are Good

When you are trying to convey information during a technical presentation, it can be tempting to show your audience lots of equations. When possible, don't!

Instead, use pictures to make your point or, if possible, animation. Yes, it might look a bit hokey, but you'll do a much better job of creating a long lasting mental image if you do it this way.

Stop With The Equation Reading

This one should be simple. If you must show an equation to your audience please don't make the mistake of reading it out to them. Either they'll get it or they won't, but your reading of it out to them won't help matters.

What Does All Of That Data Mean?

This is the cardinal sin of technical presentations: blasting your audience with too much data. If you have to present a lot of data to make your point, then at least include a box somewhere that summarizes what it all means. At the end of the day this is what your audience will remember.

What's Your Bottom Line?

Speaking of summarizing, you should do the same thing at the end of your speech: tell you audience why what you just told them was important. During any technical presentation your audience can get lost or caught up in the discussion and forget "the big picture". Help them out by bringing it all together at the end so that everyone will leave having reached the conclusion that you wanted them to get.

How To Get Ready

Preparing to give a technical presentation is just a little bit different from getting ready to give any other type of speech. One of the most important things that you need to do is to very carefully practice how long your speech is going to take. All too often technical presentations can run long and nobody likes that...

You'll also have to prepare yourself to deal with questions once you are done. The whole purpose of a technical presentation is to convey information and this always generates questions. Practice your answers before you need to give them and you'll always come across sounding smarter.

Finally, you need to make sure that you show some excitement about what you are talking about. The technical presentations that I remember the best are the ones where the presenter clearly had a deep love for their topic and it showed. If you can convey this to your audience, they'll listen to your every word.

What All Of This Means For You

There is no need to fear giving a technical presentation; however, you do need to respect it. It's all too easy to make this type of presentation boring and uninteresting. Taking the time to do it right is easy to do and the results make it worth your time.

You need to make sure that you make your presentation **understandable to your entire audience** as you start out. Help people stay with you by taking it easy on the equations and using as many pictures as possible. Where possible, relate what you are talking about to real-world things that your audience will know about.

Just having a great technical presentation is not enough, **you also need to prepare to deliver it**. This means making sure that you'll be able to cover your topic in the time provided and that you'll be ready to answer the questions that always come after one of these types of presentations. If you can do all of this, then you just may start to look forward to delivering your next technical presentation.

Chapter 6

Getting What You Want: How To Inspire Your Audience

Chapter 6: Getting What You Want: How To Inspire Your Audience

What is the purpose of having you create a speech, practice it until you have got it "just right", and then go through the mental and physical challenge of actually delivering the speech? Hmm, perhaps **our purpose** for going through all of this effort should always be the same – we want to change the world.

The trick, of course, is to figure out just how to go about making this happen. It turns out that there's really only one way – **you've got to find a way to inspire your audience**. As you might well imagine, that's easy to say, but hard to do. Maybe I should offer you some hints...

Enthusiasm Counts

How much energy can your audience detect **coming off of you from the stage?** What you say is actually less important than how you say it. If you are giving a lackluster performance or if you are just going through the motions in order to get this over with, then you're audience will detect it and there's no way that you're going to inspire them.

Find **your passion** for the message that you are giving. After that, make sure that it shows when you are speaking: in your words and in your actions.

Tell Them Where To Go (In A Good Way)

If you want your audience to do something, then you're going to have to tell them **what to do**. This means that you've got to use your speech to describe to them where they want to get to. You may not have all of the answers for them, but if you can describe what the future will look like for them, they will be more than willing to follow you.

What's In It For Me?

If you want to get an audience behind you and your ideas, then you're going to have to be able to answer the age-old question: **what's in it for me?** As you are creating your speech you need to be asking yourself one simple question: "why should anyone care about what you are going to be saying?" If you can answer this question, in a convincing way, then you will have found the key to inspiring your audience.

It's All About The Stories

I've said it before and I'll say it again: the most powerful tool that a speaker has is the stories that we tell. Our stories, unlike the rest of our speech, have the ability to connect with our audience **at a deep emotional level**. This is exactly the kind of connection that you want to make and stories are the tool that will allow you to make it.

Be Optimistic

No matter how bad things might either be currently or might become in the future, your speech needs to hold out the chance that **there is a better tomorrow** somewhere down the road. You don't need to gloss over the obvious – everyone can see tough times or big challenges. Instead what you need to do is to show everyone how optimistic you are about their future. By doing this what will happen is that your optimism will spread and soon everyone will be sharing it.

What All Of This Means For You

When we think about changing the world, we always seem to think that it is something that "other" people do. Well guess what, there is absolutely no reason why **you couldn't be that person** who makes a difference with your speech.

In order to cause a change to occur, any sort of change, you are going to need to find a way to **inspire your audience**. This isn't nearly as scary or intimidating as it sounds – yes, you really can do it.

As long as you are going to go to the effort of preparing and delivering a speech, you may as well make sure that you are going to end up **changing the world**. Take the time to do this the right way, and your audience will leave your speech forever changed…

Chapter 7

Big Game Hunting: How Public Speakers Capture An Audience's Attention

Chapter 7: Big Game Hunting: How Public Speakers Capture An Audience's Attention

In the world of big game hunting, the goal always seems to be to try to hunt something **bigger and more deadly** than you did last time. The world of public speaking isn't all that much different except that we go looking for the biggest game of all: an audience's attention.

Do The Unexpected

Face it, **we're all jaded**. We live in a world where we expect to be updated instantly via iPhone or Blackberry, we get text messages whenever something important happens, and we can get virtually any type of food within about a mile of where we currently are. What the heck do you have to offer us as a speaker that is going to cause us to pay any attention to you?

David Green is a speechwriter who has to deal with **this wandering attention thing** as a part of his job every day. He's got some suggestions on just exactly what you need to do as a public speaker in order to keep that audience of yours hanging on your every word.

First off, David suggests that you pay attention to **what your audience is expecting you to say**. Do they know who you are? Have they heard you speak before? Are you just like a bunch of other speakers? If any of these are true, then it's time to shake things up just a bit.

David suggests that you do **the exact opposite** of what your audience is expecting you to do. If they are expecting you to deliver a speech standing behind a podium, then get out in front of everyone. If they are expecting you to use 100's of slides, then don't use any at all. These types of dramatic departures from the ordinary will catch your audience by surprise (in a good way) and they'll be forced to pay attention to you because they'll want to know what's going to happen next.

Accent, Accent, Accent

Nope, we're not talking about having you sound like **Crocodile Dundee** or like you are from the U.S. deep South, instead we're talking about what else is going on on stage while you are speaking. Like PowerPoint.

How much time do you typically spend on the PowerPoint presentation that you are going to use with a speech? As much or more time than you spend on the speech itself? **Forget all that fancy stuff**, the real star of any speech is you. Make sure that if you decide to use slides that they accent (softly) what you are saying and don't steal the show from you.

It's Play Time!

So just what is a speech? If you're not careful, it's 20-30 minutes of **pure boredom** for your audience. If you don't want to inflict this kind of pain on your audience, then you've got to entertain them. I'm not saying that you've got to make them laugh (although that might be a good idea), instead I'm trying to let you know that you've got to give your speech in a way that will hold their attention.

There are lots of ways to do this. Telling **great stories** is one way to do it. Slowly unveiling a discovery that you've made is another. How you do it isn't as important as just making sure that you do it.

What All Of This Means For You

Just like a big game hunter, when you are giving a speech you are stalking prey. Your **elusive quarry** does not have four feet, but rather is sitting in a chair with four legs.

Your goal is to **capture and hold your audience's attention** for your entire speech. In order to do this you're going to have to get creative. Doing the unexpected is one way to keep them guessing – and paying attention to you. Make sure that your

PowerPoint doesn't overpower what you are saying and make sure that you tell a story or two or three.

In the end, you'll know if you've done a good job because the audience won't want your speech to have ended – **they were having a great time listening to you**. You'll know that you've had a successful hunt if you get asked to come back and present again!

Chapter 8

Four Ways To Show Your Audience That You Hate Them (Not!)

Chapter 8: Four Ways To Show Your Audience That You Hate Them (Not!)

Giving a great speech is one thing, understanding how to not give a bad speech can be something completely different. Lots of self-help books, trainers, and blogs will show you a 1,000 different ways to become a better speaker, but maybe what you really need is some suggestions on what you should NOT be doing?

<u>Don't Back The Truck Up</u>

You know that beeping sound that large trucks make when they are backing up and getting ready to unload whatever they happen to be carrying? At no point in time during one of your speeches should your audience ever hear this sound.

As a presenter, hopefully you've done some research to get ready to deliver your speech. You've probably made a lot of notes, sorted through them, and created a speech based on all of the information that you had collected. Stop right there.

There's not an audience out there that's going to be secretly hoping that you'll take more time than you've been given. If you try to pack everything that you know into your speech, then you're going to overwhelm your audience (it's like dumping the contents of that truck onto them).

Instead, you need to take the time to sort through everything that you've collected and pick out only the most important pieces that will be needed to help you make your point. Your audience will thank you for it when you are done.

Provide An Opportunity For Nap Time

I have nothing but fond memories of nap time back in the day when I was but a wee toddler. However, I've grown up and I hate it when a presenter clicks off the lights and then starts to present a boring presentation.

As a speaker you need to consider the total environment that you are going to be giving your speech in. Is it early morning and folks are not yet fully awake? Is it just after lunch and everyone is going to be settling in and, if you're not careful, nodding off?

With the arrival of projectors that are brighter than the ones that we used to have to rely on, turning off the lights in the room in which you are speaking isn't done nearly as often as it used to be. However, when it is done, you need to gage your audience's attentiveness and boost your energy to make up for any loss of energy on their part.

Tell A Story – The Wrong Way

A speech is simply a set of words that you want to say to your audience in order to create a result. Since giving an effective speech can be quite difficult, a lot of speakers like to write out their speeches so that when the big day comes, they can be assured that they'll get their words right. There's no problem in doing this.

The problems start to show up when that speaker starts to read his / her notes or, even worse, starts to read the slides that are being displayed to the audience word-for-word. Look, we can read too. If that's how you are going to deliver a speech, you may as well print out your slides, hand them out, and then we can skip the whole sitting and listening to you thing.

Wing It

If you were going to bake a cake, would you just show up in the kitchen, throw some stuff together and hope for the best? I suspect not. Then why would you ever show up to give a speech without having taken the time to properly prepare?

Just like a professional athlete speakers need to prepare for the "big game". No matter how good you think that you are, practice will make you even better. Taking the time to try everything out first will give you an opportunity to fine tune your speech and this is exactly what it takes to go from being an amateur to being a pro.

What All Of This Means For You

Becoming a good speaker (nay, a great speaker) requires you to understand what it takes to give a great speech. At the same time, you need to understand what you need to not be doing while you speak.

Avoiding mistakes such as providing too much information, allowing your audience to take a nap, reading your slides to your audience, or not practicing is the key to delivering a great speech.

Great speakers know that they need to do the right things and not do the wrong things. Avoid these four mistakes and you'll be firmly on the path to speaking greatness...

Chapter 9

Tales From The Frontline Of Speaking:
The Story Of A Keynote

Chapter 9: Tales From The Frontline Of Speaking: The Story Of A Keynote

Sure it's all good for me to go on and on about how you can improve your public speaking skills; however, what happens when I get the call to come and deliver a keynote speech in front of a room of strangers? It's times like this that everything that I've learned about public speaking **gets put to the test**. Do you want to know how it all turned out?

Getting The Call

Every speaking gig starts with a call (or an email). In my case I got an email from the folks who were setting up a meeting of product managers in Chicago called ProductCamp Chicago. They had read one of my blogs that talked about my views on product management and were wondering if **I'd be available to be their keynote speaker**.

In my case, **flattery always works**. I did a quick check of my schedule and then told them that I'd love to do it. They had taken their time in getting in touch with me: I had just under two weeks until the big event. Clearly I was going to have to move quickly.

Creating The Speech

Having accepted the offer to deliver a keynote speech, I was now faced with the challenge of figuring out **just what the heck I was going to talk** about. Although I had never met my audience before, I knew what they did for a living and the challenges that they were facing.

The organizers had asked me how much time I wanted for my keynote (how many times do you have the opportunity to determine that!). I had told them that between 30-45 minutes would do me fine – on a Saturday morning, I figured that was **just about all that any audience would want to sit through** no matter how good of a job I did.

After having racked my brain for a few days, I finally decided that what I needed to talk about were **the sweeping changes** that I believe were going to be transforming the field of marketing. If I did a good job, then this topic would catch the audience's attention and get them thinking about whether or not their jobs were going to go away. Always a good way to capture your audience's attention!

Making It Stick

Although I generally prefer a more free-form style of speaking in which I create an outline and talk from, this was a case where I wanted to make every word count. That meant that I needed to **write out my speech word-for-word**. In 12-point Arial font it ended up filling up 10 typewritten pages. I speak at about 150 words a minute and that gave me 4,973 words or about 33 minutes of speaking if I didn't speed up or slow down too much.

Having written the speech out, I now had to **commit it to memory**. I use an image / action association technique to do this and it served me well this time out. I finished writing the speech on Tuesday and flew up to Chicago so I had roughly 3 days to commit 10 written pages to memory. It turns out that that was just about right with a bit of a push on my part.

God's Angry Wrath

In all of my haste to create and memorize a speech, I had not had time to **create any slides for the speech**. I stated to feel that I needed some on Friday morning but figured that I could just slap them out on Friday night. Well wouldn't you know it, the electrical thunderstorm to end all electrical thunderstorms rolled through western Chicago on Friday evening and where I was staying lost power at about 5pm. No power meant that my laptop wasn't going to work and I didn't have any access to the Internet to get images for my slides. So much for that idea!

Things got just a bit more complicated the next morning. The house that I was staying **still didn't have any electricity** and it's on well water (pumped by an electrical pump). This meant that there wasn't going to be enough water for me to take a shower. Can you say sponge bath?

By the time I actually caught the train to go into Chicago, I really wasn't all that worried about giving a half hour speech in front of a group of strangers. **So many hurdles had already presented themselves** that I basically figured what else could happen?

One Final Trick: Just Say No To Q&A

The organizers had asked me if I wanted to have **a Q&A session** after I was done speaking. I actually really don't like those: if nobody asks a question, then I am sorta left hanging there and that's never a fun feeling.

I told them that having a Q&A session sounded like a great idea, but I wanted to **do things just a bit differently**: I'd be the one asking the questions. My hosts agreed so I took the time to create 5 questions that I felt that anyone could answer after listening to my speech.

Since getting called on by a presenter to answer questions after a speech is the second thing that I hate the most, **I came prepared**. I had stopped by a store the night before and purchased chocolate bars, some with nuts, some without. People who answered my questions get a chocolate bar for their efforts. Who doesn't like chocolate?

In the end, the speech went off without a hitch. I had no problems remembering what I wanted to say, when I wanted to say it. The audience seemed to enjoy themselves and I got many complements when it was all done. The folks who had invited me were especially grateful. They said that I had "...hit it out of the park..." and that's when I knew that it had all been worth the effort!

Chapter 10

Public Speakers Need To Know How To Work A Room

Chapter 10: Public Speakers Need To Know How To Work A Room

Getting up in front of a bunch of strangers can be a challenge for even the best public speaker. The really good ones realize that there is something that they can do about this: **change strangers into friends**. The challenge is that they don't have a lot of time to pull this off. This is when your ability to "work a room" can really come in handy...

Ya Gotta Have A Goal

So there you are. You've arrived at your next speaking engagement early enough to **mix & mingle with the audience** before everyone files in and sits down. Why? If your goal is to convert this group of strangers into raving fans, then you're going to have to have a goal.

Depending on your personality type, the event, the type of people in the audience, etc. your goals will probably be different from event to event. There is no one **"correct" goal** to have – this is a very personal decision. Possible goals can include trying to meet everyone in the audience, trying to make a few deep connections, trying to convince people to ask good questions during the Q&A session, etc.

What's Your Message?

Long before you show up for your next speaking event, you need to decide what the **key message** that you want to share with people before the event will be. The most important thing that you need to keep in mind is to not just repeat what you'll be talking about from the stage.

Instead, the message that you share with people before you begin your talk should lead up to whatever you will be talking about. If your speech is the solution, then your message beforehand needs to be **about the problems that everyone is facing**. By using this time to show people that you understand the problem, you'll be assured that you'll have their attention when you start to talk about how to solve the problem.

You've Got Two Ears – Use Them!

As important as it is to get your message across to the people that you meet before your speech, it is just as (and maybe even more) important for you to show them that **you are a good listener**. Taking the time to listen to your audience during these discussions is the best and easiest way to show them that you really do care about them.

Keep in mind that doing a good job of listening doesn't mean that you just stand there with your mouth shut waiting for the other person to be quiet so that you can start to talk again. Rather, you want to **actively listen** and ask questions based on what you hear them say. This is how you develop real connections that will cause the person to whom you are listening to pay attention to you when you are speaking.

Details, Details, Details!

The whole purpose for you taking the time to show up early and talk with your audience is to try to win them over to your side long before you take the stage and open your mouth. What's going to really make this happen is **your attention to the little things**.

When we first meet someone, **we quickly size them up**. If they come across as phony or shallow, then we discount them and move on to interact with others. You can prevent this from happening to you if you take the time to make good eye contact with people when you first meet them (yes, eye contact is important in one-on-one conversations just as in giving a speech).

Additionally, take the time to **always be smiling**. Would you want to approach someone and talk to them if they weren't smiling? This simple gesture can really help you to connect with a lot of people very quickly.

What All Of This Means For You

As speakers, we all want our next speech to go well for us. One of the biggest challenges that we always face is trying to **win the audience over to our side**. It turns out that there is an easy way to make this happen: show up early!

Making the time to socialize with your audience before your big speech can go a long way in **helping them to connect with you**. In order to do this, you need to come prepared. You need to have a goal, a key message, and you need to take the time to listen to what people tell you.

When you finally take the stage, just imagine **how much more confidant you can be**. Having taken the time to turn an audience of strangers into a room full of friends is an investment that will pay off over and over again…!

Chapter 11

The 2 Most Important Things That A Public Speaker Needs To Do When The Curtain Goes Up

Chapter 11: The 2 Most Important Things That A Public Speaker Needs To Do When The Curtain Goes Up

One of the questions that public speakers have been debating since the beginning of time is **"what is the most important part of a speech?"** There are really only three possibilities: the beginning, the middle, or the end. I'm here to solve this question once and for all: it's the beginning and I'm going to tell you why...

What Time Should You Start At? (Careful, This Is A Trick Question...)

This might seem like sorta a strange thing to be talking about when what you really want to do is to become a better public speaker, but what time you start to speak at is actually **a critical question**.

All too often as public speakers, we'll show up for an event and then we'll basically **put ourselves in the hands of the person who is running the show**. We end up saying by our actions "I'll start to speak when you tell me to start." This is the wrong thing to do.

As the speaker, you need to drive the organizer to **start your speech on time**. I fully realize that this can be difficult to do especially if as you look out over the audience there are still a lot of empty chairs. However, things will go badly for you if you don't start on time.

Just imagine this scenario: you delay your start time by 15 minutes to allow more people to arrive. They all notice that you are starting late. A break comes and you ask them to come back in 10 minutes. They end up trickling back in after 20 minutes. Then lunch comes. You ask them to be back in an hour. Most of them stroll back in about 20 minutes late. **You get the point**.

The thing that you have to remember is that **your audience's time is very valuable to them**. By not starting your speech on time you are showing them that you don't respect their time. Clearly, they'll show you that they don't respect your time either if you do this!

It's Really All About Your Introduction

Most audiences **won't know anything about you** before you take the stage. Interestingly enough, this is the same problem that professional comedians face. They've come up with a clever solution to their problem: it's called the opening act.

The sole purpose of a comedy opening act is **to get the audience used to laughing**. The opening act doesn't even have to be all that good, their purpose is to get the audience warmed up and ready for the main course: the headlining comedian.

In the world of public speaking your speaker introduction plays the role of your opening act. It is through your introduction that **the audience's expectations will be built up**. Not only should your introduction explain why you are here, but it should also lay out what you'll be talking about.

As you have probably already guessed, your introduction is **too important to be left to chance**. Some speakers leave it up to the host of the event to come up with some clever words to say. This is like playing the lottery: sure you might win, but the odds are stacked against you.

Instead what you need to do is to **prepare your own introduction**. Type it up and make sure that it covers why you are the right one to be at this event talking about this topic. A key point of a successful introduction is to have it lead up to your actual speech so that the transition from the introduction to your speech appears to be very smooth to the audience.

What All Of This Means For You

As speakers we all want each speech to go well. It turns out that we are really **in charge** of how things turn out. We control how each speech starts. To make your next speech a success, there are two things that you must do.

What we need to do is to **set things up** so that our speeches always start on time. Doing this communicates to your audience that you respect their time and that they should be sure to return the favor and respect yours. Your speech should start with someone else introducing you. What's important about this is that the introduction is your opening act – it sets the stage for what you are going to be saying. Therefore, it needs to be done correctly. Never leave your introduction to chance – write it out and provide it to the person who will be introducing you.

How a speech starts sets the tone for everything else that you have to say. Taking the time to make sure that **you get off to a good start** is the key to ensuring that your next speech is guaranteed to be a success...

Chapter 12

It's All About The Introductions...

Chapter 12: It's All About The Introductions...

Did you know that how well a speech is going to turn out can be determined **before you even open your mouth?** It turns out that introductions are one of the most important things that that set the tone for a speech. If done correctly, then you're going to have an easy time coming out on top. If not, well then there's just no way that you can win...

Introducing – You!

In a perfect world, you would have someone introduce you before any speech that you gave. **Unfortunately we don't live in a perfect world**. This means that all too often we find ourselves in the awkward situation where we have to introduce ourselves. When this happens (and it DOES happen), you need to be ready to say the right things.

The trick with this kind of introduction is that you need to walk a fine line – you are special and the audience is lucky to have you there to give a speech, but you really can't come out and say that. Instead, you are going to have to find a way to **allow them to reach that conclusion all by themselves**.

One of the best ways to do this is to use your self-delivered introduction to communicate **your passion for the topic that you will be talking on**. By taking the time to explain how you came to care so much about the topic you will be able to show your audience that you know what you are talking about and why they should listen to what you have to say.

Introduce Your Audience To Each Other

If you want your audience to pay attention to what you have to say, you're going to have to find a way to **make them feel comfortable listening to you**. One rather unique way to go about doing this is to halt before you start your speech and get them to do something for you.

What you are going to want to have them do is to stand up and take just a moment to **introduce themselves to the rest of the audience**. Of course the size of your audience matters – if it's too big, then you can't have everyone introduce themselves to everyone else. However, for smaller groups asking everyone to share their name and one other piece of information (where they are from, why they are there, etc.) can be a great way to change everyone's view of your speech.

Instead of showing up and sitting with a bunch of strangers to listen to a speaker that they don't know, **something will have changed**. Now they'll be sitting among people who they know and with whom they have something in common.

As a speaker this will work for your benefit. Everyone will be in a more relaxed and positive mood as you speak. You should find it easier to connect with your audience and **they should enjoy your speech more**.

What All Of This Means For You

As speakers we are always looking for **ways to better connect with our audiences**. One great way to make this happen is to use the power of introductions to start things off right.

All too often we'll find ourselves in a situation where we end up **having to introduce ourselves**. When this happens, we need to be careful to not come across as being too boastful. Instead, share with the audience why you care so much about the topic that you'll be talking about and they'll understand that you really know what you are talking about. Likewise, taking the time to allow your audience to introduce themselves before you start to speak can help everyone feel connected.

When we meet new people, we always start the relationship by introducing ourselves. As speakers we need to find ways **to use this social skill during our speeches** so that we are able to better connect with our audiences and thereby more easily change their lives...

It's from the forge of failure that the steel of success is formed.

Hard Work Does Not Guarantee Success, But Success Does Not Happen Without Hard Work.

- Dr. Jim Anderson

Create Speeches That Motivate Your Audiences And Get Your Message Heard!

Dr. Jim Anderson is available to provide training and coaching on the topics that are the most important to people who have to speak in public: how can I create a speech that people want to hear and how can I deliver in a way that will allow me to connect with my audience and get my point across to them?

Dr. Anderson believes that in order to both learn and remember what he says, speakers need to laugh. Each one of his speeches is full of fun and humor so that what he says "sticks" with everyone.

Dr. Anderson's Public Speaking Training Includes:

1. How to plan your next speech: pick your purpose and understand your audience.
2. What's the best way to get PowerPoint and Keynote to work with you, not against you?
3. What do you need to do when you are presenting in order to truly connect with your audience?

Dr. Jim Anderson presents over 100 speeches per year. To invite Dr. Anderson to speak at your event, contact him at:

Phone: 813-418-6970 or
Email: jim@BlueElephantConsulting.com

Blue
Elephant
Consulting
Speaking. Negotiating. Managing. Marketing.

Photo Credits:

Chapter 9 – By: Dr. Jim Anderson
http://www.BlueElephatnCosnulting.com

Chapter 10 – By: Dave Chiu
https://www.flickr.com/photos/scoobyfoo/

Chapter 11 – By: Phil's World Travel
https://www.flickr.com/photos/philsworldtravel/

Chapter 12 – By; 드림포유
https://www.flickr.com/photos/124961070@N02/

Other Books By The Author

Product Management

- How Product Managers Can Grow Their Career: How Product Managers Can Find And Succeed In The Right Job

- Product Management Secrets: Techniques For Product Managers To Boost Product Sales And Increase Customer Satisfaction

- Product Development Lessons For Product Managers: How Product Managers Can Create Successful Products

- Customer Lessons For Product Managers: Techniques For Product Managers To Better Understand What Their Customers Really Want

- Product Failure Lessons For Product Managers: Examples Of Products That Have Failed For Product Managers To Learn From

- Communication Skills For Product Managers: The Communication Skills That Product Managers Need To Know How To Use In Order To Have A Successful

Product

- How To Have A Successful Product Manager Career: The Things That You Need To Be Doing TODAY In Order To Have A Successful Product Manager Career

- Product Manager Product Success: How to keep your product on track and make it become a success

- Marketing Skills For Product Managers: How Product Managers Can Use Marketing To Make Their Product A Success

Public Speaking

- How To Become A Better Speaker By Changing How You Speak: Change techniques that will transform a speech into a memorable event

- How To Give A Great Presentation: Presentation techniques that will transform a speech into a memorable event

- How To Rehearse In Order To Give The Perfect Speech: How to effectively rehearse your next speech to that your message be remembered forever!

- Secrets To Creating The Perfect Speech: How to create a speech that will make your message be remembered forever!

- Secrets To Organizing The Perfect Speech: How to organize the best speech of your life!

- Secrets To Planning The Perfect Speech: How to plan to give the best speech of your life

- How To Show What You Mean During A Presentation: How to use visual techniques to transform a speech into a memorable event

CIO Skills

- What CIOs Need To Know About Working With Partners: Techniques For CIOs To Use In Order To Be Able To Successfully Work With Partners

- Critical CIO Management Skills: Decision Making Skills That Every CIO Needs To Have In Order To Be Able To Make The Right Choices

- How CIOs Can Make Innovation Happen: Tips And Techniques For CIOs To Use In Order To Make Innovation Happen In Their IT Department

- CIO Communication Skills Secrets: Tips And Techniques For CIOs To Use In Order To Become Better Communicators

- Managing Your CIO Career: Steps That CIOs Have To Take In Order To Have A Long And Successful

Career

- CIO Business Skills: How CIOs can work effectively with the rest of the company!

IT Manager Skills

- How IT Managers Can Make Innovation Happen: Tips And Techniques For IT Managers To Use In Order To Make Innovation Happen In Their Teams

- Staffing Skills IT Managers Must Have: Tips And Techniques That IT Managers Can Use In Order To Correctly Staff Their Teams

- Secrets Of Effective Leadership For IT Managers: Tips And Techniques That IT Managers Can Use In Order To Develop Leadership Skills

- IT Manager Career Secrets: Tips And Techniques That IT Managers Can Use In Order To Have A Successful Career

- IT Manager Budgeting Skills: How IT Managers Can Request, Manage, Use, And Track Their Funding

Negotiating

- Learn How To Signal In Your Next Negotiation: How To Develop The Skill Of Effective Signaling In A Negotiation In Order To Get The Best Possible Outcome

- Learn The Skill Of Exploring In A Negotiation: How To Develop The Skill Of Exploring What Is Possible In A Negotiation In Order To Reach The Best Possible Deal

- Learn How To Argue In Your Next Negotiation: How To Develop The Skill Of Effective Arguing In A Negotiation In Order To Get The Best Possible Outcome

- How To Open Your Next Negotiation: How To Start A Negotiation In Order To Get The Best Possible Outcome

- Preparing For Your Next Negotiation: What You Need To Do BEFORE A Negotiation Starts In Order To Get The Best Possible Deal

Miscellaneous

- Software Defined Networking: Design and Deployment, CRC Press 2014

- The Internet-Enabled Successful School District Superintendent: How To Use The Internet To Boost Parental Involvement In Your Schools

- Power Distribution Unit (PDU) Secrets: What Everyone Who Works In A Data Center Needs To Know!

- Making The Jump: How To Land Your Dream Job When You Get Out Of College!

"How to put together a speech that will capture and hold your audience's attention"

This book has been written with one goal in mind – to show you how you can organize a powerful and effective speech We're going to show you how to make sure that your next speech clearly communicates your message!

Let's Make Your Next Speech A Success!

What You'll Find Inside:

- **BACK TO BACK TO BACK TO BACK SPEAKING: HOW TO**

- **YOU CAN LEARN TO SPEAK LIKE PRESIDENT OBAMA**

- **TECHNICAL TALKS: IS THERE ANY WAY TO MAKE THIS STUFF INTERESTING?**

- **THE 2 MOST IMPORTANT THINGS THAT A PUBLIC SPEAKER NEEDS TO DO WHEN THE CURTAIN GOES UP**

Dr. Jim Anderson brings his 25 years of real-world experience to this book. He's delivered speeches at some of the world's largest firms as well as at many conferences. He's going to show you what you need to do in order to make your next speech a success!